AF323210

A LONG ROPE AT THE EDGE OF THE VOID

Douglas Blazek

EDITION
MUTA

Grateful acknowledgment is offered to the editors of the following journals, in which several of these poems first appeared in earlier versions: *Acid, Allegheny Star Route, The Ark River Review, Arts in Society, Aspen Leaves, Assembling, Bartleby's Review, Borderlands, Chicago Review, Circular Causation, Coldspring Journal, The Dragonfly, Dwang, East River Review, The Falcon, 48th Street Press, Free Lunch, Free Poetry, Galley Sail Review, Gegenschein Quarterly, Gravida, Greenfield Review, Grist, Hearse, Hunger Enough, In*tense, Invisible City, Kansas Quarterly, Lillabulero, The Little Magazine, Longhouse, Long Pond Review, Lummox Journal, The Malahat Review, Meatball, Measure, Monument, The Nation, The New Salt Creek Reader, The North Stone Review, Oink!, One Trick Pony, Orange Bear Reader, Pinchpenny, Ploughshares, Poetry Now, Prism International, Quercus, Quetzal, Rattle, The Red Book, Remington Review, Second Aeon, Second Coming Anthology, Strinktree, Suernos, Thee Flat Bike, Tool, West Coast Poetry Review.*

Eichmann appeared in earlier versions in the following anthologies: *Poets West: Contemporary Poems From the Eleven Western States,* Perivale Press; *Leaving the Bough: 50 American Poets of the 80's,* International Publishers.

The last four poems constitute the 48th Street chapbook: *The Song That Ends Ends Our Singing.*

Published by Edition Muta
www.editionmuta.com

FIRST EDITION

Paperback   MUTA 08   ISBN 978-0-9850044-1-5

*For my father, whose love is a braid
of heartfiber holding me above the void.*

*And, of course, for Rachel,
my seamstress of safety nets.*

Contents

"Taking a political position is and remains the decisive test.
It is what reveals the ultimate meaning in philosophy."

– Vincent Descombes

"The victim breeds the brute."

– Maryse Choisy

Patriotism

If not for that damn
flagpole stabbing me in the eye
I'd be able to see.

Uses Of A Flag

To twitch atop the last leafless
tree atop a hot treeless planet.

To blot the last bled oil spurt
out the last hemophiliac pit.

To sop the last splat sludge
from a lip-leapt alphabet.

To stuff the hole in our chest
from the last ideological bullet.

To trap the last computer chip
back empty-handed from its trek.

To wrap the last atom of air
ashen in the atmosphere.

To lash the earth to its axis
then whip it till fixed.

To savagely wave surrender.

Like-Thinking Is Right-Thinking

You worked for presidents.
Invented brooms for a twitching brain
to whisk away contradicting witches.
Dickered in the closets of corporate popes
swapping priapic troglodytes in undercover robes.
Sold your soap to the status quo
to sanitize infectious paradise.
It is said you were a Wall Street surgeon
implanting dazzling spasms
a button could control.
It must be true.
You are so popular.
Now that you are president
you press us, the people, to work for you.

Dear Mr. President

Your death is a monumental
prod to condom-clouds.
Your fame swollen and cocky
in the anus of the earth.

Your death is the epitaph
of pathological polygraphs.
All those zigzag lies
mapping-out the zeitgeist.

Your death is indistinguished
unlanguaged exsanguinated
grass crawling a land
an insect with glasses digests.

Election Night

Radios are statically
deciding who is president.
Trees are procrastinating
a polluted choosing.
Lightbulbs overhead
electrocute their elements.

Hopalong Cassidy could
be king, for all I care.
Hell, Vinegar Bend Mizell
scored a seat in Congress.
Used to pitch for the Cards
back with Harry Brecheen
and Howie Pollet.

I do not remember their motives,
how they threw the curve
or who their victims were.
I only remember the terror
of placing an x in a box.
My body standing at home plate
holding a stick of wind.
Another statistic.

Midget Official

Every day on my way to work
a stubby ruddy dog
snaps and growls at me,
the enemy, with Socrates
in my pocket.

Every morning,
without question,
this pest
preps his overprized
endocrines,
his power-prone
endorphins.

Every afternoon
he patrols the propped up
shed, stocked with hemlock–
a grog for gossip's
noggined qualms.

Every evening
he shits a bone down
a mouth of dirt.
Then growls as it plots
against him.

He guards, of course,
his dog flesh
best, that gorse
greed of meat
basting in his oven's
pavlovian sweat.

He is boss of the box.
Brash as the X
barked against ballots.
But, as luck elects,
too hung over
from lapping his testes
to leap the fence.

Theory Of Economics

A worn coin circulates
my pale veins.

It will buy the last pair of shoes
at the Salvation Army.

It will buy a dead cabbage
and a spoon.

I enter the store and place
my arm upon the counter.

The clerk draws his knife
professionally across my wrist.

Finally the coin is extracted
and I go about my business.

On the street, my convulsive paucity
squeezes its peristaltic pouch.

The courthouse reeks of catatonic heat.
Legal hell keeping hot the atavistic soul.

Cabbage will cook throughout the years.
Its steam gagging the scream of history,

that mobius burlesque
justice reluctantly auditions for.

Tomorrow I will walk and never stop.
You will find me at your doorstep

banging my spoon against
a drum of air.

The Multitude

They are buzzards.

In solemn pandemonium
they enter emporiums
indulging and engorging
beaking the meat of merchandise
ravishing the fashions
sinned by mannequins.
They need just one thing.
Eat. Eat is what they need.

If tempted by razzle,
you won't rest.
The buzzards will track you
with x-rated bait
nuzzling your face.

They will besiege your bed.
Fleece your sleep.
Peck the slut of your eyes.
Heat your blood to hot saliva.
You will itch and burn
and be hostilely hungry.

The buzzards will strip
your skeleton
to this: $.

Glut Of Privilege

We are done with the sea.
With whale, shark and squid.
Done with the earth.
With elephant, skunk and snake.
Done as a roadside condom.

Dump them into a sack.
Dump the sack into a pit.
Dump the pit into the dark.
Dump the dark into the past.
Dump the past out of context.

This is not cartoons on holy
temples. This is sequel depleting
the repeat we accumulate.
This is math vanishing aftermath.
Affluence looting sacrament.

In Praise Of Profits

All the clouds are fleeing their womb
to escape the sky's matricide.
They need you!

The wind has died.
They need you to weep them
over the land.

There will be no water
no crops
no hours
without your help.

It is not too late.
Yet in harness you
haul a vault of numbers
to accumulate more tumult.

It is not too late.
Yet, airing the prayers
of have-nothing millionaires,

you bribe more ciphers
to make more blinders for empire.

Treason

We scope her echo
cloning the tones
our satellites own—
360 degrees
of digital infinity—
infography clogging
holography's imago—
a craving accrued
to a crude malfusion—
the beauty of her music
a shaman's brutality
any mammalian technology
must reign.

Rockets to her chakras
rip her epiphany's
auric apparitions
staining our forebrain.

They nick the ark
but not its visitation.
Scatter the spores
of Bach's lightspeed
evolution.

Across the desert.
Dragging a cello.
A hole in a cradle.

Figures torque their imprimatur
through the lure of infinite ink.
To absorb the book at the end of space.
To overturn each page.
To blot its amorphous ledger marks.
To deconcoct the cosmic rorschach.
A puckered skull is sucked
for the kiss of richest knowledge.
Virginity of genesis
chipped into a Kriss Kringle sack.
Vaginal navigation, empty
as destiny, now features conartistry
colonizing cold ovarian icons.
A messy pleasure measuring its marquee.
Now playing: The Epic of Ejaculation
From Here to the Zodiac!

Pioneers Of Space

Monotonous elaboration
eons out of elements
time-notched thereabouts
cellular fears stalled in bewares
throne-tooled gears
turning to topple the cogs of gods.

Cacophony sorting chaos
ratcheting an eyelash out an atlas
angling strands of entanglement
to avenge the plot of dna
to knot control of a socket's optics
rope-wrapped round a roving rock.

Vats of swaggering nanobots
machines preparing tarot scenes
vascular antlers greasing their heat
speeding the spew of metallic sperm
wrangling an impasse of light
teeth scrimshawed with seraphim

empire-men hauling-in the moon.

Progress

Wind is coming.

A frictional wind.

Ticking against a petulant whetstone.

Soon the future is too sharp to touch.

Velocity straight as a razor stroke:

trees shaved to a nazi stick
pencils docilling
rows of headless decimals.

Peril calculates perished air.

Erased space
escapes
through the nick in time.

We make it happen.

We make everything happen.

We make matter suffer
to make suffering matter.

16

We make the nail for the natal hole.

We flash percussive tungsten
over chromium grass
over selenium hills.

We swell our corporeal caul
over skeletal girders.

A storm. A city.

Thrust through every molecule,
shrieks of fire trucks
race to save the blazing ravage
outrage and overjoy
throbbing their nozzles!

I check the street expecting
to find the city in flames
but see only beams, haloic
in mist, shadowed nods
conducting chapel-traffic
oddly unradical, melodically old.

Approaching the desk, I sidestep
my dog tucked deep in dog-sleep.
And if I kicked her with a word
then sat to riot craft out my pen
rape-feeding truth its medicine,
what right would be crime?
How American! Tumorous freedom
looting-to-own! Voting for harm!

Instead I script the infinite arc
of a star's first letter,
the brow that allows an eye's
phrased-in exposure.
An aperture evolving
my following optic ink.

A luminous alphabet
connects imminence
to what beckons it.
Startles self-portrait
in a lexical mirror.
Neverbefore metaphors
entering their end intent
by route of periphery
until entering is all about.

Tonight I imagine revolution
committing the vision
that recruits its own use.
A music renascing its changes.
Vibration in riot arriving
insighted. Not a siren
but velocity of a city
synchronizing crisis
with the emergency of Light.

...And Yet In Great Fervor We Build More Fires

Heat sits, squats on roofs
softens shake to licorice
cringes cattle, chimneys
their knees, cooks
a species to whiffs of gristle
scalds trees crusts cats
embers the wingless
breeze in birds
gasses cars to ghastly
briquettes praying to charcoal
on their heavenly way, bakes
talk to casket calk
broils oil-spoiled
pleasure domes
sealing tombs
with official seal fumes–
Promethean dreams'
sky-writ screams
gagged by sleep's
atmospheric mattress
stuffed with wealth's
prestigious ash
torched by Tekhne's
unbeatable glee
force-feeding us
more corporate scorch.

How To Change The World

A gun appoints
the world's dead end
your mentor,
projecting crux
upon the screen that extends
through everything.
A squeeze of trigger
releases an infinite
alphabet: rubik
instructions to hit
your useless future
with a universe
never used.

You have options:

Aim elsewhere.
Aim inward.
Load with transparence.

Is Is Everywhere, And I Am Growing Old

I cannot make up my mind:
either revolution
detonating my armchair,
or technological slaughter
by atoms with no emotions.

Winter excreted heaps
of headlines, and now
their stalled stink is thawing.

Can I forego my eyes'
reliance on solvers
brushing out the aftermath
of sky's Lascaux?
It is sad, I know, craving
logos in a cave
as it echo-roars away—
jets in extrospect
painting sunset's ripcord
opened long ago.

There are handgrenades
in my grapefruit.
I am not sure of the target,
but, if I eat,
where do I duck?!

After The Marxist Rally

Handbills abandoned at the curb
billow a moment
with a life frightful to see:
brittle political dandies
circulating their damaged family
posing as a mobius halo
round a murderous make-believe.

A Volkswagen putts its godspeed
commotion, two green kayaks oceaning
its back, as a yellow Ford's one blue
door dolphin-slips round a corner—
off to sun-oiled homes, shoes
eased into closet slots, spiders
trapezing from curtains to cabinets,

hair gagged in scabby drains,
flies smudged on window screens,
stitching machines and straight pins
subduing a uniform afternoon,
spent screams from boardgames
snug in the same room as grandma's
old world snoring— weary immigrant
safe in ordinary sacrament.

O revolution! Go hang yourself!

War is civilized in the city:
battle orders bullhorn-blasted
up the arse of anarchists.
Crisis hiked to chaotic odds
crushed by eyeless touchdown gods.
Punts and passes and savage tackles.
Yardage lost for divine regain
while one floor down this traumatist
hacks and thrashes the attacking air
crashing chairs through wife and walls!

Revolution loosens demons
uber reason and uber all. Screws
resolve to demolish the sewers.
To rally humanity's anality
around an E. colic apocalypse.
But, after his flush flooded
the floor, he fisted his feces
into the face of the world,
shat the canards of a narcissist,
then collapsed in a catatonic huddle...
and the crowd and the cops
and god all cheered another score!

Raising A Family In Consumer America

I have never heard a bird
seen a bird
birds are behind enemy lines
chirping tiny violence

it can be blamed where sperm went
the flesh whose kiss was abyss

consumers investing
in manifest destiny
making minerals merchandise

tyrannic identitarians
rutting Jurassic
die-cut dice
forging
the riveting roar
that runs an empire

my head is reptile for feathers
their absence digesting hereafter
holiest terror of god-grunted blood
dumped into the hollow of a nest

I wear a costume of jet
but flap a heap of sweat

I fly
in mock escape
watch this winged man
cross the war zone
existentially spent
approaching the mercy
of a mountain!

A bird. Scouting
about. Travels
a route unraveled.

Drops. Dies.
I watch it rot.

Songful no longer, its
tattered systematics
dissolve in breath's prow
progressing in place
its novice navigation
toward the source
of matter's nostalgia.

Structure's
effacement
utters nothing's
unutterance
escaping
out possibles
just stopped.

A tinnitus scrimmaging
with logical cacaphony
to reorchestrate the cogs
lost in molecular
chorus.

I twist a wisp
of wishful turnkey.

Toss to air prayer's
embedded specs
stretching what connects
from nature to now:

all quarks informed
by harmonic harm
brought forth
unquarrelling
so force can alter
score to paramour.

Vibratoed Om
behind the scenes

ever echoing
before
things are things

quickens extremes
to the quick of intrinsicness
issuing keys
to techniques in ubiquity
kneeling a species
anew in music:

a knell replayed
by revisionist ears
on a player bird
by sacred players.

Pathology Of Monday

Stuffed with gift-wrapped breasts
sweat-festered suits
unproofread looks
spiced with brutal body sighs
the train attacks the tracks.

Clackety fractured glass:
street after street of infected
brick: defective truth
a broom pushes its bristles through
sweeping the trash of irrational history
down alleys of contagious reality.

A morning's sortie to the top
stops where a profit's toccata forges
a course to force apart its harpsichord.

Does surviving echo's cacophony
mean counterpoint's C.E.O.
must master the control of ventriloquy?
If music's destination is its notes,

what tune will approach its orchestration
to recruit the hero of the uncomposed?

Freeway Graffiti

Unhearted rushhour artery,
drone-frozen insects

radar-beamed, swarming home.
Bump-snore grump at 4 a.m.

Undecorumed trucks
transporting brand-named dreams.

Wary rattled wares trojanly
preparing the day's betrayal.

Faux-razed overpass
besieged by sprayed emergency.

Rucksack placard-flash
whizzing a winced eye.

A blanched ambulance screams
past. All stops crossed out.

We grip the "now" of asphalt
but are bullied on.

Suddenly the freeway ends
in unhurried sod and weed.

All around is burial ground.
Miles and miles of speed.

Building The Ruins

While viewing the new plaza—
fountains spurting crystal ambergris,
stainless sinless towers
poised as immortal fashion models—
I saw skid row.

In bed, heatedly asleep tossing about,
I sense owls annealing my absent beak
leaving its meaning in secret vowels.

Night glass, mirroring an eye's
self-image, shatters to electrify
a city. A guillotine sweeping pieces
of sheen within my head
to extract from it the unexpected.

One day, like lightning in a dream,
I will bolt perfectly upright
and snare one of those birds.

The Toy Gun

A mother reflexes
extra heartbeats at metal-

makers, her chapelbelly
distraughtly
recalling the fetal

astronaut
who once floated there—
his other-worldly

solipsistic sweetness.

Aiming his tin plaything
he lasers
her mock fist
with a cocky blast
of gland-command.

Those controlling somatic
no's, whacks
photographed by crowds,
stored as a hornet's
hyperbolic

sting
coiled tightly
in pre-rowdy jittering

then freed with a bang
from that buzzing
old brainstem.

The child grins as if sin
were warting
his potence like magical
toad sperm.

Ancestors weave
khaki sorties
into his paradisical
TV. Whatever strategy
his desires seize
they plagiarize
the world's demise.

Already this babygod
is blasting up the shaft
of skyscrapers,

up the *uber alles*
of penthouse space.

Up to rape stars.

His pitch is to sell
the light he can't catch.

To buy what he sells.
And fall where it lasts.

34

They Come To Us

Knocking at our door.
Every day. Dressed as bait.
Slick crooked shapes
slipped to a hook of mirror.

Such suckers. We answer
every time. Bath sponge
in our hand. We answer
with the amnesia of surprise.

Paradise crassly preening
in the casket of their valise:

bottles of pink sublingual skulls

gregorian perfume that waits its chants
then rips apart our oxygen

recipes for razors braised

a therapeutic electrical device
implanting castanets in our flamencoed head
has no switch
never turns off.

They come to us as a succubus
blurting bloody non sequiturs in our pulse.

Hoping to catch us unprepared.
To sell a zealous entrophy
decaying need to creative chaos.

Leaving their consolation card. Promising
to call again...

We have feet
therefore we talk.

We have words
therefore we fly.

We have lies
therefore we hide.

We hide in our enemy's eyes
therefore we cannibalize.

There is nothing more to relate.
It is settled.
The world will proceed.

The Camera

Conceal it in the bedroom
behind a smudge on the ceiling.

Surround it by the contour
of your bathroom mirror.

Its show of shots will expose
your pose plotting in your closed closet.

You will never hide in the skin
of your flipside again.

In time of war install
cameras everywhere.

Their apertures will capture
your antagonist secretly your fraternist

fabricating a freeing treason
collaborating within your dreams.

Planet Cannibals

Gulping a wrist's in extremis
run. Rivers ripsucked.
Thirsty free tickets

to liquidate pulse.

Nature
rapaciously slave-sired
by celebrity science.

Wealth in a vein
maimed by its aftermath.

Usual rubics
gouging geology's
holistic plurality.
Horizon flatlined
to well-urned allure.

Grandiose callousness
assaying the corpse-effect
of sunset's decay.

Rayless helios
heedlessly

spoiled
by well-oiled

vocations—

profit's
failed upscale palace
storming above us

in unreinable
reign.

Never enough
never weathers the cost
of meteoric
carnivores.

Fuhrers
of antecedent's
afterlife

in furious
release increase

their speed to eat
what a species

self-eats.

The Butcher

This priest of meat praises
the weight of it, lays
his thumbs' compulsion
upon its prophetic nakedness.
Fetishly pets the kill
to tame death's kleptomania.
To forestall his jealous
mortality from being severely
spiritualized. Defiantly
his eyes re-kill with a whack.
Boys leave their mothers for this.

Cleavers are his lovers.
At sunrise he sharpens each
against his teeth, shines
their inner virginness out.
Shaves his body of bristle:
suspicious animalness
concocting the mock bellicosity
rabbling his penis.

His apron is sexed in blood.
At night the gospels sweettalk
him to bed, rapt in erection sweat.
Sleep is steel without grip.
A slide of slippery strokes shearing
breath to sliced hereafter.

Singing Low In Stuck Roar

Gods jet in polygraphic clouds.
Sunrise is dowsed by jagged white lies.
Mops gag at the mob-splotched floor.
Shops unlock their prosperous obstacle.
Amnesia repeats its contagious panacea.

At work we gaff our laughing heart.
Crank our raucous chainsaw talk.
Complain of pain's delayed escape.
Paychecks stuck in prayed deflate.
Mercy cursing its sawed-off crutch.

Home heaves its song low in the throat.
Sings for a heaven of beef and peaches.
Sings as a bull asleep on a truck.
Supper sets its trap of hunger.
Terror swallows its perpetual roar.

Appetite

> "Humanity is what it eats."
>   – Feuerbach

In the café words eat words. Greed
eats greed. Infanticide eats infants.

Flocks of silverware are snared mid-air.
Coffee arrives in a khaki cup.

Potatoes are gagged in battle-mash.
Roasts admire their quagmired float.

A throat is stroked with ambient
vibrations of a shiv-shaped violin.

Next a city, a cute pet-of-a-city,
is mauled by eating-etiquette.

The proof of a future is chewed
like evidence in a paper shredder.

Finally air is clear as starbreath.
Peace is thicker than exhaustion.

The words are finished eating.
Nothing remains but the words.

Slow-Motion Cataclysm

Sinking our incisors
into obesity's beef,
we eat the Cro-Magnon
mystagogue's dream.
Here, enthroned on this omened
tar pit, this asphalt
Styx, our Sistine
fingers clutch the celestial
payoff, the holiest moment
a shaman ever stole from stars.
We read of mammoths in Alaska,
how Burger Kings in Yukon Creek
serve steaks of those ancient
beasts, cataclysmic events
dropping them
dead in their tracks,
undigested buttercups in their guts.
Species, survivalized,
saliva-lied into deep freeze
thawed as commodity.
An entourage of wiles
follows our gods
recycling their smiles
in miles of wilds
lobotomized.

We digest all mass.
Our mastication's
aftermath
stuffed in sub-spherical
cracks
cheering
all acts of acquisition
quaking exorbitant
self-absorption
demanding
more datum and zen
axioms, techno
slang and shogun
slogans, omens
imploding
down
the compelling
expelling
ink-trinketed
sphincter
all stink.

Watching Television

Grandma's in the kitchen
stretching membranes, simmering
cabbage in a pot of magic,
slurring a burr of garlic in.

She clamps the grinder
to the carving board. Sets
an old crock bowl to settle
an old impossible score.

One hand crams the ageless
mouth with blundered chunks,
the other turns the tail
forcing sausage out the hole.

She sings of grinding brides
and babes. Powerful louts
and chameleon priests. A Polish
mother's weak Te Deum.

With an abrupt muffled laugh
she takes a common pestle
and roughly stuffs the skin
tight as triumph on a tv screen.

Kielbasa and kapusta. A howl
of nutrition christened by steam.
A taste of skewered truth our
taste buds squirm to taste again.

Captives Of Saliva

Across the tablecloth: the fashionable
slaughter. A hatchet's flexing
handshake applauding a pleading neck.
Species cracked apart, cackling
vile prophecies out a sky's uncanny sack.

Splotches of ketchup. Gruesome
curds of guffawing coup d'etat.
Wads of embattled gray contagion.
Hunked muscle in crumpled linen.
Intimate gristle from invisible wars.

Tomorrow chlorophyll will exhale
the embalming fluid of our talk,
and trilobites will reason above the roof.
Shards of plates will scratch the sharks
eating the sea's deepest aphrodisiac.

Our robust lips industriously suffer
the palimpsest kisses of Rome.

Sausage Thought

Saliva as salvation
heaven's insufficiency
stuffed in what is stalked
fluffed in sacred fragrance
shuffling off as dressage
undressed by sausage thought
eaten as a sentence
repeated into wastage
brain's ball and chain
bullroaring its circumference
kitsched to a culture
killing for its cure.

Goya Could Have Painted This

Next door my neighbor
massages his car with a mass
of diapers and a fussy muscle.
Pumps a gush of disastrous past
into the zoom of impassable future.
Speeds his freeway personality
pitching cliches to periphery
selling recycled carnality
as demons round a rosary.

His trees are green nonentities.
Roses grip masochistically
his sadistic chainlink fence.
His politics makes power stink.

I would rather eat hooks and electricity,
chew a quarter mile of chrome,
than live in this slum of prosperity,
but wherever I am Mr. Everywhere goes.

Goya could have painted this
but not with a brush.
Goya would have stretched our skull
to the dull diode glow
of a Sony canvas, then broadcast
our monstrous success as Pavlovian
reflex eating more resource
to gorge our abyss.

Goya would have shaped
this screen's inescapable tomb
to the Ultimate Lumen's
spreadsheet revenge.

Goya would have thrown
a bolt of black lightning
back through the brain
of wince thou came
down our throat's
historic peristalsis
to rut our origin
squalled in the smell
of a wrong god's wrong end.

A circuit consuming its flow.
A cannibal's self-fellatio.
Zero's art of zero.

Fire Sermon

Collapsing! Cataractally
past the roof! Sky-axed!

Elm stunned! Limb cracked
out a tree's synapse!

A snarl of bees. Dust barbs
stuck in a porous gag of buzz.

Hours later they recharge
in the margins of routine.

A mortician with chainsaw
begins nibbling the fringe,

invading its tasty memory
of suckled light and savored rain.

Then all that remains is coma.
And so the bees come home.

Sunless. Moonless. They
cluster like electric seeds.

A truck drags their un-nouned
sound to the scorching ground.

Gasoline is splashed and a match
struck— time just squirms.

Fate consumes its salivary fuel
suffering lumination.

Ricochet cremation. Radiation
escaping. How history keeps hot.

Mankind, hiding in height,
shaking a tin of thinking dice,

preaches their legal nature.
Feels, as extinction is signed,

the regret of an avalanche
overseeing its victims.

Brilliant Night Without Moon

Anxious tree branch
scribbling the roof,
wind taking its hand
talking it write.

What sayeth forecast?
Knowing would be pointless.
What could a tree
teach the creators of megadeath?

Trees To Reveal The Centuries

Trees have expensive memories.

Civilization imbedded
subatomically, toxic

quantum clocks circulating
their alarming rings
round casket

desks
where technocrats,
snug in wireless earplugs,
underwrite

the progress of impasse.

Spectrographic horoscopes
scratch last rites
across defiant math

gawked on chalkboards,
stored in all the formulas

of pictorial orators pretending
the Oz of a false
positive is emerald evidence

a colossal proof
will miraculously bloom
out our fossiled future.

Nature's Cretaceous
deja vu, everywhere
crucial, no cruise control–
a volatile tale well-
charted to sell

untold carbon
to a dark cartel.

Speed's etherteeth,

addicting its richest
lips to chainsaw diction,
speaks the digital
consumption

of astrophysics
blackholing
the spectacular specks
that run everything–

earth's
ghostly sack
of growth-ring chips
gone
to macho history

cashing-in.

Too Small To Matter

Across the turbulence
a snail glazes forth
foraging the carcass
of prosperous drought.

A man affixes the fetish
of his face above the artificial
fields and scientific mist.

"I am the post-green," he grins.
"The hierarchy of reality."

Such trick retracts the transitional
yet feigns to mimic it.

"I am the utopia of utility!"
he cries, his chi trapezing
his freewheeling belief.

Nodding an inaudible
godspeed without scold,
the snail leaves a kiss.
A seed for eavesdropping lips.
Feast for the process

that devours the flute
to evolve its music
out a wooden cocoon.

Archeology Of Romance

Hoisted up a shaft, half-optical
half-vertigo, my cheeks
brush strata

after tarsaled strata:

bystander
beast
pounced by beast
pounced
by appetite's

divine right.

In higher strata: steel
scree of empiric vertebrae.
Fossiled techtonic
monorust. Monstrous
redux of rebar and girder
retched and shat
creeping in towering crouch–

and I am hoisted still higher

up into the explanations:
muscle trained by fear–
the persona of a fang
intruding predation
through stageskin
to make the wound the play

ordains.

And somewhere still above,
an avalanche
re-sets its leverage.

History,
jotted in our genes
from atop a plot of time,
tons down

our tautology
through an artery's red stiletto
carving bits
of silhouetted language

bleaching their recursion
into consciousness.

Is it this
that makes romance

ossify
its a priori
lovestory

crushing the art
of discovery the other

sculpts of us?

Critical Mass

> "Ancient myths tell that the world
> has been destroyed and recreated
> four times by terrestrial catastrophes,
> and that each time humanity has entered
> a higher stage of consciousness."
> — Frank Waters

Deceased soil, oil flogged, leaking
black anatomy out a bag of spoils.

Sorrow-spoors, once wheat
once oats, swallowed into prayer.

Silent rags of cyber threads
spread to net their siteless master.

Morning climbs its scaffolding
laughing down at ruined heaven

bickering to rebuild its burst
with civil bricks of hydrogen.

Closed-circuit lips creep their politics
into crypts of syntactical distraction.

False clocks of mimicked tics
trick-tock their metastasis.

A world collapsed upon its mass
quakes a makeshift quasar gas.

A tardy star, startled dark
out its cadaverous chrysalis,

paints its cave's imagination
unchaining its imaginer's chain-reaction.

Corporate Ocean

Ocean waves running in... an old muse
young again

running in... running in...
splashing news of plankton
and the extra of a dancing turtle.

Shells flash in the sand handfuls
of freshly glazed pastries.
Gulls peck a piece of alluring dross
to feed an implacable clan.
Sealight glares its other-worldly
wonder into planetary air.

Today in Cambodia
child-brains are creamed
and curried with the homilies
a dictator drips from a spoon.

Today in Nicaragua
a minefield of mangoes
explodes its traumas
pitting and pocking
the vanishing point
of pointillistic sleep.

Today in America,
an armada of asphalt
paves the sovereign sea
securing pacts for foreign disaster
luring leaders to prosperous defeat
supplying coke and fries
for protest's beef,
incorporating opposing
waves to make
all tides obsolete.

A Shore's Urgent Sea

Carved by a backhoe's
rusty buckteeth,
these beachcabined cliffs,
hexed with prosperity,
stare hard at the sea:

how waves heave yet hold their heaving
in potentiated *fait accompli.*

How dreams, sinking
in a sleeping ship, are seized
by undersea ventriloquy.

How sound, torn in tumbling,
is restored so suddenly
to music's internal enormity.

How a rowdy obbligato
throws its crescendo
toward all that surrounds

then timidly
retreats on belly
of cellophane, leaving
constellations of brine
holes, blue weeds

and sea fleas,
a clear slide to catch
the carcass
of every savior consumed.

This coast, once sovereign
self-homage, now suffers
trash drums and food fat, sand
tanned by a merchant heaven
vending its ovened sun.

Metallic jolts of radio-rock
blast their emotional
wreckage out a manic-
aggressive

digital syringe
convulsing adrenalin
to the vassalaged brain

while a man scrotumly
scratches his flaccidity

while a woman butters
her pungent flesh then tongues
the rip in the raft
of her mouth
exposing the words

that puncture.

Impotence

Old men rock upon the porch.
Their genitals stone dwarfs in a sack.
Memory a maggot scavaging its absence.

Poetry amuses till its music kills.
Its half-life a secret pact
with what occurs before its happens.
A flare inflating the ionosphere
to illuminate its diffusion's view.
A catalyst commingling afterwards
with the change that furthers everything.

But why old men?
Why swish the mouthwash of Lazarus?
Want to hear about the hanging?

It was cold that night.
Cold and wicked
as a simple sacrifice
bold enough
to make a cripple whole.

They slipped the loop around
his neck and suddenly he looked
less a poet and more a pope.
His bones a cathedral's I beams.
His mind the ancient matrix
of intersecting paradigms.
Whipping drool to atavistic lather,
they yanked him through the moon.

They got him. The one who
extremed the sky to violin its light.
Who decoded the motionless core
appled within a rapid orchard.
Who married his masculine
glass to a womanly mirror.
They got him! They got him!
Goddamn muthafucker
was rutting up our fear!

Frontier Ballad

They catapulted thrill into kill.

At first it was rock. To mash
it to blacktop.

Then trees. To beat greenbacks
out beatific green.

Rivers leaped freeways in attempt
to retreat, but sewer
pipe tripped their escape.

Air tried to scream but oxides
from engines up-stuffed its throat.

They killed children.
Their weapon was fame.
Sportscocks and filmqueens
eagerly embalmed
in a spotlight of skin.
A love-me orgasm
desperately sustained
on the screen of the brain.
It was merely a flash
but it was everything.

When everything died
there was nothing left.
Rock was dead. Root was dead.
Water was dead. Weather was dead.
Was dead... Dead. Dead.

Only a colony of killers was left
clinging like wasps to a globule of fat.
Everybody's ass in somebody's mouth.

Treacled ingots of sun-fecalled caskets
secure in assets of dusk.
At last they were stinking with wealth.

The Prayer Star

One star. Sparked
off the whetstone.
Directing sharp shaft
bright into death.

Stretch of an eye:
perpetual theft.

Tip of heaven
festering investment.
An arrow's prayer
in our praise of settler.

Magic Mushroom

Welcome year 1945
in gorgeous Alamagordo.

Welcome that wild chanterelle
atop our skull's campstove.

Now we can cook a town down.
Trade morel ornament
for shitake monstrosity.

Spooky mushroom soup
brewing in the caloric limbo of our kettle.
Carrot-crisp children stirred-in
with celery trees and potato dwellings.

We pepper rhetoric
to antagonize the antagonist.
Salt self-similar assault in his mirror.

Time now for the entree
to kowtow in our maw.
For the pop-up genie
to gobble its formula.
For nuclear psilocybin
to themepark our mind.

For radium's tailspin
to thrill-ride our requiem
through anthracite awe.

Through savorial slaughter
to unavoidable void.

Through planetary bowels'
sopranoing lamb.
From pylorus to cloaca.
Babes, all of us!

Psalm

The easy part:

Horror crams its belly laugh
down every trembling crevice.

Playgrounds gasp the sound of vastness.
Weeds and trees burst into spirit.

Houses heave on heat-ashed asphalt.
Sky a scald of merchandise.

History's climb ignites its height.
Faith in hierarchy a fahrenheit traitor.

Skulls expel their spellbound vowels
that vowed to end unendurable terror.

Voices wave as strato-vapor.
Prayers kiss their gods goodbye.

The difficult part:

Survival is not
an arsenal of glands

but the shine
that shares

the sheerest mirror
other wears as Other.

Seeing sight
in eyes

that wish
to annihilate
us

altruizes
surprise.

Orange Kills Rainbow

Torn by bombs of ancient
orange, arboreal gods

inflame the storms
of imposter democracy.

They thrash at aircraft.
Swallow pustule bullets.

Gag-suck gut-sauce.
Trip-wire maps back

to the taproot desk
where death's first general

strategized metastasis.

Democracy In The Empire

The war is always the same:
skyscrapers vs. mud huts.

Gridlocked cars, armed with bombastic
debt, threatened in the company lot, placard-shout
"BOMB THE BASTARDS!"

Strategic jets
snag the sky's
threadbare fabric
intercepting the mending
stitch of a star's
infinite art.

Crying is seeing.
It makes the ribs grow lean.
Such is winter, here, where trees
are unusually thin.
In the land of voted
everything.

Homeless After The War

Nowhere out a boxcared
shove, this man
with muscatel stagger

mutters half-words split
by the lash
of official signature.

His life is his daily bait
writhing on the hook he bites.

His thoughts an accumulate fume
evading the abrasion of a match.
Kidnapped by khaki,

his flesh is flashback
trampled in frontal attack.
Subsisting off malls,

the acquisition he trusts
is trawling for trash.
Of all history's infallible
tales, his is the last we tell

yet the first the bell of liberty
patches into its cracks.
Seeking victory, it can be seen

thumbing an asphalt treadmill
dogtags wagging
tolling the hole the fallen fill.

Pity The Sons

Under-sheet pearl shots,
tusks in virginal musk,
girl-gods scored and notched.

Sport-blasted rabbits,
their corpse a habit
of retold sex sorties.

Boys that swore at steroid
toys beefed their biceps to score
the father that authored war.

But there are no fathers anymore.
They stalked the wild elevators
to fuck the posthumous top of sky.

We see them thinning through t.v.
printing their fist on the universe,
their smile terse airport gin.

And we, the sons, stab nightly
the night-stake through their chest:
a festering antenna of nothingness.

What Happened To Satan?

We are angels. Skeet-shot by mastercrats
blasting vassaled genes into our fleecy squeaks
grinning the same savage x that savored Auschwitz.

This day is history's plea in the p.s. left off page:
death retracing its steps out its technical
never and not to rerun the setup that ran amuck:

power plants churning paradise to well-urned smoke,
business-grit whittling it to a necropolis,
polar caps stretching to clap their sloppy fists.

We are angels. Shoveling all our shot-to-hells
into the furnace of the tallest bank on earth.
What a blast we get investing in heat.

Ilse Koch

Death by rope.
A million fists frayed
to twist round her neck.

Her scaffold request:
more prostrate men!
More hemorrhaged revenge!

A jiggled glass rod
savage up your cock.
Then staggering sex
of Nazi kick and knock.

Harder. Then harder yet.
Vultures clenching your brain.
Clawing and beaking each strand
of pink screaming meat.

A blurting man
bonds you to the trough,
your body bottomed
on the slops
and spurts of blood.

Pious on our knees,
we fit beneath our tongue
the pit that pulls her feet.
We endure the torture

of her glassy stare
swallowing with no relief
the look that shatters
our last belief.

Eichmann

He enters tactically
to shut off the gas
and electricity.

His eyes loose
in a bad socket
shocking innocent light.

He is determined
to shut it off
even if I were locked
in a machine
that ran my heart.

"You are on a list,"
he says, statistically.
"It means nothing
this life in you.
This flute braying
its weak music."

His business is order.
Compressing chaos
to an inflexible fist.
He insists:
sixty six dollars
and sixteen cents.
But all I can do
is stare at him
as if he were the universe.

82

The Falling Staircase: 9/11/01

Each on a separate step,
together. Self-invested leverage
anonymous in dominant loft
aggressively pleading
release from steel's irremedial grip
too manifest
but to fall through flaw.
Flames reflex-reaching
to polyethylene heaven
out the mosque of collapse.
Toxic black oxygen
boiling in living skin.
Nerves shitting their limits
ratcheted beyond urgency
a body can bear.
Screams begging in a paralyzed
screech to ease somehow
the intolerable thing
too endless to ever cease.
A cloudy hand held in trust
now too ruthless to ever touch.
A stack of stories extorting
the froth of truth
sorted acquittally by history
too two-sided to choose.
Such prosperous ruin
forever up-looking–
the stare of justice uselessly there:
invisible blueprint
to build the next stair.

Of Last And Lasting Things

HUMAN SORROW, I
round your surroundness,
its long-coming omen
opening gone moments again.

HUMAN SORROW, my
eyes ingress your script
to strategize the complicity
a skeptic seer can see.

HUMAN SORROW, you
stick my midpoint pointing
direction: center's daimon
aiming pain through pain.

HUMAN SORROW, I
add your scattered abacus
to what cannot add up
counting aught loss begot.

HUMAN SORROW, you
admit to authoring the pity
ethos and eros escort
to the court of your abyss.

HUMAN SORROW, my
death in you exists
to kiss your exit-depth
eclipsing what emits.

Survival Poem

We brained him with femur bones.
He tore our skull to the core.
We raged at the howling surrounding us.
Cooked food in a farther spot each day.
Our teeth canny as the unnamed.

This year we pray to cyber sutras
computing the end of truthless use.
Appropriate the universe
from satellite dish to solar plexus.
Crux our brains with a nugget of static.

Survival was once adrenalin and awe.
It saw no sun but shadow.
Now survival rivals all it knows.
Serums of ciphers expel cyanotic noise.
All ganglia is shared paranoia.

A circuit banters through synapse.
Births boastful volts, but its shock
flops back to the iconic past.
Survival moans.
Telecasts its coma to outlast what lasts.

The world's wealthy catastrophe to date
has purchased ministers, examiners and fate.

Fortress-force in torso-wars scores
morbid hoards of morsel-corpse.

Forebodes the savage foreclosing chorus
sing-songing across the course of language.

Forges skin's foreglimpsing script
brailling genetics from repetitive lip.

Something obedient vs. something that bleeds.
Something of speech eating its speed.

Something unspoken removing the tongue.
Something adaptive vs. something undone.

Crosshaired Crucifix

Coming home without yourself,
what truth can exit polls exhume?
What mandatory story of a win deformed?
A vote if not for war is not American.

Teddy bear skewered at barbecues.
Bare ass basted by cannibal elders.
Testes molested by encephalled dreck
ritually nibbled by a Baptist witch.

Selective Service did not pussyfoot
snatching touchdowns from dad's penis.
The family crisis high on sacrifice
trophy-gloats on the status stage.

Opium kisses skin's crematorium
dreaming more than dreams afford
questing a system of shamanic questions
to resist the lust of a crosshaired

crucifix chestblasting justice.
Whacking protest from the roof.
Just commerce. Proof
of reaching the untouchable top.

Battlefield Syrup

Adios without orchestra
no matter
how songful we are.
Without dance
no matter
how fancy our steps.
Can we coax
x-bombs
to domestically
fry eggs?
If not, the jig's up.
So, christsakes,
lie down, take a nap,
smoke a pipe

split a melon.
A crucifix flexes
the hex of its ruse
doubling the trouble
its double-cross accrues.
Tutors butchery
to squeeze a battlefield
to the syrup of industry.
Forges morality
into the mortality of more.
Hacks nature
to an atlas of scars.
Cuts and pastes
genetic ownership
into clustered code
out a genie jar.

So here we are,
turbulent in urban roulette
jackpotting fashion's
mirror-as-mansion
chancing our throbs
to mob a mall.
Pallbearers staring
as gangster-gods
grafting looks
to a class above stars.

Fixed in victory's
vicious avariciousness
we trade trite agonies
for payoff catastrophe.

We amass safety
in saturate fat.
In adaptive math
gadget-feeding
our metallic intellect.

We spin
however still
we stand.
We fall
despite the drop
we stop.

Survival's scared,
earthly scarce.
Seas are seized
by greed debris.
Air rivaled
by vital denial
cybering higher
than a pile of tide.

Locused focus
loves its onus
aiming aimless
out our anus.

We do our part
exporting our name.
We do our part
extorting for gain.

So sit down. Smoke
a pipe. Slice a nap.
Inside a melon
parts of dreams
are the severed
same sweet thing.

Obscene Astrology

Our society is sick.
Everyone says.
It is sick. Every
society is sick.
No bread.
Just ovens.
We butter the dust.
We crumble our tongue.
We sponge tears from our spleen.
We cheer the king as the king
robs us of cheer.

We repeat
the meat-whack
of ancestors. The next
axe. The next wheel.
Progress impeachable.
Pieces of god shat to landfill.

Raping by mania
we copulate fantasia.
Text-by-text atrocity
births the sacred
ox of orthodox death.

All around us.
Too slow to see.
Copywork of busyness
buries our speed.

A master race
takes its master thief
to fake a masterpiece
for the patent office.
Law applauds,
dropjawed,
a whore as before.

Self-similarity's
identical twin
doubles its datum
round the prayer
mirroring its wheel's
revolving mirror.
Just wind-up fun.
A toy a banker
sells his son.
A trick wish
spinning its top
to vanish its bottom.
A surface that is chasm.

Our cities are sand.
Byzantine blind.
Sub-seismic grain.
The fall the funnel
forecasts its castles for.

We paint ourselves
with a bristleless brush
into a cornerless cornering
stockmarket truck:
steers steering steers
to wall-less slaughter.

Yes. Our society
is sick. Sick
as gristle in skeletal
rift. Self-cannibal
wholesaling a global oven
financing the heat
of our Fahrenheit paradise
baking us
in the revolt we eat.

Stinking up the zodiac.
Everyone says.

Power

When that old debut construed
itself it lawed all calculus.
Kludged the logics of opposites.

Appointed the hours' surrogate
power to pock impeccably
through innocent traumas of air.

Chthonically managed by a quantum
mechanic, a messianic panic
apes the fables of a messy planet.

An apple, babbling in an orchard
storm, loves its torture
rebelling to quell its swelling norm.

*

Men in military orgasm
bang home. They parade
terrain with landmine eyes.

Cock disaster at breasts
erotic. Brag a contract
for acts psychotic.

Love's aperture, choking
heroic prostheses, breeds
a future of fetus grief.

*

Vulva's impulse-jelly
burns with greedy sperm
heating obedient genes

flaming brand-names brains
raging to own the remains
saved from nothing gained.

*

Sinewed sonar's rear-viewed
fear revives sieg heil droning
its sorrow ever dead ahead

stored in tomorrow's carnivore
insinuated in every signature
voted by remote control.

*

Atop the towering abyss
our rapelling minds
climb to claim all everests

falling back to attract
their forwarding force.
Grasping it as it grasps us.

Evolution

Task in vacillation. Testy sea gas
thundering at gelatinous terrain.
Radium's mass caprice of morphic etch.
Cosmic luck exploding yoke-slush.

Why should this crouped heaving
rally gardenly stratagem?
Conclude as personality?
An algorithm of cell astrology?

Maximal crimes of endocrinal masters
convolute to rule the fundament.
Adrenalin assailing veins. Harm untamed.
No brakes. No breakthroughs. No tune.

Who is brain-talk? Who broke the chastity
belt to exponential language? Cracked
the locks to electromagnetic magic?
Torqued the tongues of synergistic sacristies?

Failed superiority makes stalemate stories
re-calibrate their gain, makes power's
vulgar prayers rampage nature
authoring its corpse into luxury mulch.

Tools of fragmental wholeness
awl through thought's all,
making a sieve to see
what sprints synaptic aperture.

Questions evolve complexity.
Reconnnaissance, affinitied
to infinite depth, transcends
annexion of conscious quest.

"If art throws its readers into a state of crisis, it is doing
its job."

– Susan Sontag

"No true artist will tolerate for one minute the world as it is."

– Nietzsche

Forthcoming from Edition Muta

Uses of Being Animal

my dog has the face of a great man.
His eternal pestering sperm
is the envy of evolution's posthumous plan.
He does not barter away his paw
for clever sleight-of-hand.
He does not knot calamitous threads
to catch what captures his casted net.
He does not plot to consume the sun
to sit on the throne of its backdrop.
Somehow he has said what there is to say
in one short snappy sentence
tenaciously repeating it
to sharpen his teeth.
He does not climb a plummeting rung
to profit from the loss of the highest plum.
He does not hire a chauffeur of laws
for his claws are off-road short-cut justice
He does not caulk titanic leaks
to float the historic past
or jerk the leash of progress
to provoke its breakneck dash.
He is his own audience.
Having gnawed through applause,
he is free.

AFTER WALKING TO AND FRO
AND UP AND DOWN IN IT

Douglas Blazek

Each book by poet Douglas Blazek now being published by Edition Muta represents his life's work. However, it is not a mere reprinting of what was previously published in his 50-plus years of writing. Each, instead, is a complete revisioning accomplished through a 25-year process of re-writing, repeatedly, year after year, the original versions.

By mid-point in his writing life Blazek had published over 1000 poems, collected in over two dozen books and chapbooks, appearing in over 400 journals including *New Directions, American Poetry Review, Chicago Review, Poetry, TriQuarterly.* His editing a literary magazine *(Ole)* and publishing a small press *(Open Skull)* in the 1960's helped to free poetic restrictions and give impetus to the alternative publishing manifest in so much of today's poetry output.

Blazek is recognized as a primary instigator of the
Mimeo Revolution – a course correction for the culture,
dedicated to "making poetry dangerous". In this
endeavor he was instrumental in publishing formative
work by Charles Bukowski, d.a.levy and Robert Crumb
alongside other poets and artists central to the era.

Despite such prominence, Blazek describes the obligation
he felt to his poetic evolution as a *"self-lit fuse detonating
its own limits.*

*My poetry demanded to be fully realized, just as elements of nature
cannot be less than their inherent design. Knowing the futility of
achieving such perfection, if I were not to address what I had previously
published, the kinetic imagination of my early writing would merely
serve as an inferior prelude to a more successful later work that
advanced by observing its participation in the mirror of its creation.
In synthesizing those potentialties into their self-requested destiny, I
catalyzed a process that allowed a timeless dimension of ripeness
to exist in all my poetry.*

*Over the years, new poems were spliced into the manuscripts I was
rewriting. My poetics accelerated to sketch its dialectics on the synaptic
scrims of reality in a language of paradoxical correlation, suggestive, yet
simultaneously skin specific— unitary in consciousness. An inked cohe-
sion of mysterious signatures informed by an all-encompassing vision.
No old poem is old. Each is as fresh as if never breathed before, yet
preserves the bones its body first owned in its natality. "*

The book now in your hands is neither representative
nor atypical of his other efforts. Neither chronologically
early nor late. Early and late are all in the same matrix,
all a portal to Blazek's life's work.

Edition Muta titles

Douglas Blazek:

Aperture Mirror

Gutting Cats in Search of Fiddles

The Blindfold Alphabet

Ventriloquy of Light

Foolish Visions

Vanished Pursuit Into A Remembered Future

Wallace Berman – In Conversation...